# COCO SINATRA

*poems by*

# Laurie Barton

*Finishing Line Press*
Georgetown, Kentucky

# COCO SINATRA

## ACKNOWLEDGMENTS

I to wish to thank Jessy Randall and Dan Shapiro, editors of *Snakeskin
UK*, The Music Issue (May 2023) in which "The Dawn of Personal Music"
appears.

I also wish to thank Susanna Clemans and the writing group that meets in
her home.

Publisher: Leah Huete de Maines
Editor: Christen Kincaid
Cover Art: Pamela Smith
Author Photo: Pamela Smith
Cover Design: Elizabeth Maines McCleavy

Order online: www.finishinglinepress.com
also available on amazon.com

Author inquiries and mail orders:
Finishing Line Press
PO Box 1626
Georgetown, Kentucky 40324
USA

# Contents

## THE AGING POEM
*—A dialogue with ChatGPT*

Q: Why is aging so hard?

A: Money—how much do you have? Is it secure? So many have so much more, your dentist, for example. The famous have infinity pools. How long will you live? Longer, perhaps, than your checking account. And remember the job you had forever? Like a little brindle dachshund you had to put to sleep. You miss the squabbles and bosses who die, one by one. Next is your brother, and then it's your shiny blue car.

## ORANGE COUNTY REAL ESTATE BLUES

You worry on the phone with a mortgage broker describing some monster at 10 percent interest. You collect bank statements, asking the teller if she likes moving. Yes, she does—a chance to get rid of things—you think of bags splitting in your closet, fuzzy sweaters you never liked. Someday, you'll toss them, though where will you be? You wander townhomes, dodging boys that race electric bikes. You pity battered condos that look like cheap motels you cannot leave. You envy single family homes, sitting like princes protected from traffic, hidden by Hong Kong orchid trees.

## SONNET OF AMICABLE DIVORCE

You don't drink on Saturdays
but that doesn't mean you can't light
up the brain with a bowl of creamy
fettuccine and peas, or sit with him
watching the harbor, munching on
chunks of Impossible Burger
mixed with a portion of greens.

Nor does it mean you two can't enjoy
the mansions on Cliff Drive, making
architectural observations that once
sparked hopes of a beautiful home,
future as fake as the acrylic nails
you wiggled before him, white-tip
proof that you were pretty.

## LEFTOVER PIZZA, EXHAUSTION

Imagine leaving a nightmare
and trying to create a perfect home
with bath bombs and silk blinds
and splashes of Red Bull
all over the divorce papers

Wouldn't you reach for a salty snack too?
Steaming pepper and pineapple
crust as soft as the pillow lost
and shrunken
in the new machine, soft

as a touch, doe-gentle
and curious, no banana
stickers spotting the walls
or mold spreading
on the floors like blood

## THE SENSATION-SEEKING POEM
*—A dialogue with ChatGPT*

Q: Why is alcohol so addictive?

A: To you? It's the brain you were born with. It gets the GABA going so you can relax. Then it tickles you with long blue feathers at the circus of reward. More and more. In every store, you know which aisle. At every bar, the flag of taps. It helps you enjoy the people you study. And forget the heavy boots.

## SIPPING A HAZY AT THE SANTA PUB CRAWL

Girl in a short skirt
dazzles in boots, cranberry
sweater slipping off
shoulder

After merry vodka
bombs, she'll be dangling
a blacked-out
presence

All the demure ones
cuddle with dads
of the future. Sequins wink
on Santa hats

that crown the espresso
martinis. My earphone
birdsong softens
the chatter and boom

Alone in a pub
with you in a condo
feeding bacon pizza
to the dog

Our old home cold. Dust
in the spot
where ornaments
used to glow

## COCO SINATRA

No one walking but me
on a rainy Tuesday, walking
all the way to Helmsman

No one on the patio but me
and my dripping umbrella
folded like bat wings

No one chuckling but me
when I see what the brewer
concocted this month–

Coco Sinatra, an agave
dream, diamonds dipped
in suntan oil

that first chilly sip of martini
a dusting of bright desert stars
as I am flown, to the moon

# RENOVATION

This spring the privet blooms    without me
pinkish hint of May   the riot to come
blushing reminder     each year's bashing
   of hopes

The condo has rental potential   dirty
cupboards    torn from walls
rusty sink    gone missing

I miss the spaghetti    the garlic bread

At the kitchen window   I study lush shade
the ficus     that persuaded me
    to stay

You smell    as you talk to Juanito
vinyl planks    mahogany    the knotty
pine you only like   in cabins

Juanito     patient as stone
asks for thousands of dollars   to do
    what you ask him    to do

We two have cut   all canoodling
our closets bare   our clothing stripped
but I swear

there's a lingering    glimmer
you mention heartwood    steely dead
   heart of a tree

## STALKING AN OLD CRUSH
## IN LAKE COUNTY, CA

He looks the same, really.
Slim and strawberry blond.

Except that now, a couple
of degrees distinguish him:
soil science, the cultivation
of vines.

His wife, a walnut farmer.
A boy and girl adopted
in big-hearted chastity,
who knows?

It's plain to see that we
are not a match. I kill plants.

I like my nuts caramelized,
tossed on a cloud of whipped
cream. Will talk about anything
but nitrogen, bees.

## DINNER WITH GONZALO

Turns out he's the son of famous
parents, a dancer and a mariachi
master. Met him through my brother,
thinking he might become enamored
with me. Now I see he was simply
polite, offering to share his avocado
toast, asking how many freeways
I'd taken to reach the dusky mountains
where they played jazz. Who falls
in love with a grandmother in baggy
golf pants? He took his bread
pudding to go, nodded good night
as the summer moon pined
a minor key.

## THE ICON BOND

Two pillows, doubled up for rest,
fluffy in front of me.

I strip off my wine-colored smock, lay
it flat like the flag of a defeated country.

I hop on the still-firm mattress
to watch a spectacle alone:

how an abused girl from Canada
bought herself implants.

Married a bad boy, got herself
kicked while holding their baby.

Still so sweet, she comforts me.
Two breasts like pillows

inviting my dreams, love
and wings, soft like me.

## HEATHER, LOOKING SLIM
## IN KHAKI SWEATS

Yes, your face is puffy
and bland, white dough

and yes, your lost expression
tells everyone

you are not well, and it's true
you walked a ledge

in very thin flip-flops
but still, your body

bodacious as ever
the diets

you count on, tequila
for dinner, whatever

you rocked
in your calendar days

## PRISCILLA AND HER BEAU

The times they stayed in bed
for weeks: lysergic acid,
pajamas on fire

Pillow fights turned violent–
naughty photos, poodle
pups

Sleepy blondes in a blur
and that darkened room
she left to discover

the world, and found him
again in divorce court
holding his hand

## HE IS NOT HERE
*—Matthew 28:6*

The angel told two Marys
not to be afraid, as guards
turned stony, like the dead.
They ran from his lightning
brightness, toward Galilee
to tell the broken men.

The angel told two Coreys
in Hollywood not to trust
the business. One lived
to prove him right. The other
died of pills, as cold as any
guru at the end.

The rumor spread that His body
was stolen, to perpetuate the myth
of resurrection, the one we have
to die to understand. Neither Corey
wore a cross, displayed no pain
of hanging there.

The surviving Corey shares his
story, the two Marys long gone
as the Los Angeles freeways
fill with lonely people trusting
nothing to get them through
the wilderness of miles.

## DUMPED BY TEXT

A friend of thirty years
didn't like my fervor
or my doctrine.

She must have asked
her shrink to craft
the message:

*I am making new commitments*
*that will keep me indefinitely*
*busy.*

*I hope you will enjoy the support*
*of those who can honestly embrace*
*the beliefs that you cherish.*

No more discussions of Mexico
City, or how to pair empanadas
with Argentine wine.

No more promises to read
and critique her essay
on mastering Spanish.

With all my best wishes, I loved
her *thank you* with a feigning
little heart.

## DEMENTED GNOME SPOTTED ON NEPTUNE

I saw him on the corner of Neptune,
whizzing by, demented gnome
on a dented bike.

A few days before Halloween
I told my brother it was over,
so glad

to be the cat that landed
neatly on her feet. Escaping
a freak show, he said.

Speaking of him
for hours a day, looping
the lavender path.

Away from him, sweating
awake into fall, to gusts
of a ruffian wind.

## EXTRICATE YOURSELF

That's what my father said, as I fell in
with a gang of schemers and druggies.
He knew they were bad high school news.

It's worse for me now, closer to his age
of pre-dawn death, surrender, a simple
shift for the night nurse.

I want him to pull up in a moving van,
stand at the foot of my stairs
burly forearms crossed

stronger than the baby-faced cops
who get called when I am not punched
but blocked in the hallway

faced with shouts from a twisted
bearded mouth. I want his gripping
magnet eyes to pull me out.

## THE RUNNING BACK

He made it as far as the wife
and three kids, a lake home
and surfing in Fiji.

When the new sprinkler system
didn't work, he sobbed. The notes
on the website didn't make sense,
nor did the streets two days later
when he forgot where he was,
lost as an ant on the moon.

*Everyone's stressed about Covid,*
they said. True enough, but he
suspected his bell was cracked
from too many tackles, too many
occasions of getting it rung.

He found his way to the hospital
parking lot, to the shade of a
lodgepole pine. *Think there's
some trouble in spot 32. Someone
hunched over–something is wrong.*

His words, the last woman
on earth. Turned off the phone,
and steadied the pistol. Knew
it was time to outrun.

## A GUN FOR VICKI JO

She did what you could have done
on one of those bad bad nights.
She wiped him out in his sleep
with pops that sounded to her son
like slamming doors.
He thought it was another fight
and rolled over into a dream
as Mommy drove blind
to a friend who didn't believe
but finally saw it was true.
Where was the friend
when she locked the door
and shot herself in the right eye?
Why so many fetters
of cheating and bitters
and gin?

## WHY DID GOD MAKE YOUR DAD SUCH A JERK?
*—for Juliette*

The question he asked you. At six, you knew he hated
himself, expecting you to hate yourself, too.

He smashed his lips on yours and stole something
you were saving for a boyfriend.

Pointed between your legs and laughed, telling
you not to think you were awesome.

Yanked the string of your Little Mermaid bathing
suit top, said you had nothing to cover or hide.

Nothing, the word you finger at night
the nothing you feel in the dark.

## ADVICE FROM SNOW WHITE

You get more buzzed on IPA,
she told me, as we compared
our favorite brews

Never mind that it tastes
like dirty socks, or turns
your belly fat, or gets you
making out with strangers
in a flooded laundry
room

She straightened her black
wig as I squeezed myself
into the Dopey costume,
both of us thinking
of bottles like gods
awaiting the end
of our boring parade

## DANCING WAS EVERYTHING
*—with lines from "Cherry Bomb" by John Mellencamp*

Our hearts
were really thumping

The rusty hope
of farm boy rhythm
perfect for rocking
alone

Thinking how you could
groove to a fiddle and swing
me around

Yes, we were young
and we were improving

# THE DAWN OF PERSONAL MUSIC
*—Sony invents the Walkman in 1979*

Foam-cushioned ears, bookish
eyes on grapevines whizzing by.

No more begging the radio gods
to dispense the balm of favorite
songs.

The singer's plea: *one day out of life
it would be, it would be so nice*

One day becomes a century's turn–
grapes to wine, love to children,
losses.

Our tapping feet declare
a holiday to every listening
city. The future climbs
like a ripe vine.

**Laurie Barton** is a Pushcart Prize nominee, Best of the Net finalist, and winner of the New Southerner Literary Prize in Poetry. Her work has appeared in *juked, Glass, Bending Genres, Lunch Ticket, Jabberwock Review* and *Snakeskin UK*. She holds an MFA from Antioch University Los Angeles and received a scholarship to attend the Disquiet International Literary Program in Lisbon, Portugal. She lives in southern California and teaches English to speakers of other languages.